JAM JAM JAM

with
THE EAGLES

CONTENTS

ON THE CD

The CD is split into two sections; section 1 (tracks 1-8) is the backing tracks to the titles listed above. Section 2 (tracks 9-16) is each of the backing tracks listed above with all the lead guitar parts included for your reference played by Stuart Bull.

WARNER BROS. PUBLICATIONS - THE GLOBAL LEADER IN PRINT
USA: 15800 NW 48th Avenue, Miami, FL 33014

WARNER/CHAPPELL MUSIC   NUOVA CARISCH   INTERNATIONAL MUSIC PUBLICATIONS LIMITED

CANADA: 85 SCARSDALE ROAD, SUITE 101   ITALY: VIA M.F. QUINTILIANO 40   ENGLAND: SOUTHEND ROAD
DON MILLS, ONTARIO, M3B 2R2   20138 MILANO   WOODFORD GREEN, ESSEX IG8 8HN
SCANDINAVIA: PO BOX 533, VENDEVAGEN 85 B   SPAIN: MAGALLANES, 25   FRANCE: 25 RUE DE HAUTEVILLE, 75010 PARIS
S-182 15 DANDERYD, SWEDEN   28015 MADRID   GERMANY: MARSTALLISTR. 8, D-80539 MUNCHEN
AUSTRALIA: PO BOX 353   DENMARK: DANMUSIK, VOGNMAGERGADE 7
3 TALAVERA ROAD, NORTH RYDE N.S.W. 2113   DK 1120 KOBENHAVNK

First Edition 1996
© 1996 International Music Publications Limited
Southend Road, Woodford Green, Essex IG8 8HN, England
All rights reserved

Music arranged & produced by Stuart Bull and Steve Finch. Recorded at the TOTAL ACCURACY SOUNDHOUSE, Romford, England.
Stuart Bull: guitar & drums, Gerry Cunningham: bass, Pete Adams: keyboards.

Introduction

The TOTAL ACCURACY 'JAM WITH...' series, is a powerful learning tool that will help you extend your stockpile of licks and fills and develop your improvisational skills. The combination of musical notation and guitar tablature in the book together with backing tracks on the CD gives you the opportunity to learn each track note for note and then jam with a professional session band. The track listing reflects some of The Eagles' most popular recordings, providing something for guitarists to have fun with and improvise with, as well as something to aspire to.

The first eight tracks on the CD are full length backing tracks recorded minus lead guitar. The remaining tracks feature the backing tracks with the lead guitar parts added. Although many of you will have all the original tracks in your own collection, we have provided them in the package for your reference. The 'JAM WITH...' series allows you to accurately recreate the original, or to use the transcriptions in this book in conjunction with the backing tracks as a basis for your own improvisation. For your benefit we have put definite endings on the backing tracks, rather than fading these out as is the case on some of the original recordings. The accompanying transcriptions correspond to our versions. Remember, experimenting with your own ideas is equally important for developing your own style; most important of all however is that you enjoy JAM with THE EAGLES and HAVE FUN!

From the Mid-1970s to the start of the 1980s The Eagles held sway as one of the great rock bands of the decade. But while rock was the group's forte, they blended elements of folk and country into many of their songs. The Eagles evolved from the folk and countryrock movement that sprang up in Southern California in the late '60s and early '70s. None of the four founding members were native Californians, but all eventually settled in Los Angeles because of the musical environment.

Bernie Leadon had a huge interest in folk music which caused him to learn guitar and banjo before he reached his teens. Leadon played with local groups in Florida in the mid-1960s before heading to Los Angeles in 1967, where he worked with a series of groups in the late '60s. Rand Meisner's career began in his teens with local groups in the Midwest. Later, in Los Angeles, he was a founding member of Poco with Richie Furay and Jim Messina.

Glenn Frey grew up in the more frenetic pace of urban Detroit and after dropping out of college, he moved to Los Angeles. Hanging out at the Troubadour club, he became acquainted with Don Henley. Henley liked to play drums, but wasn't sure of his career direction. He finally heeded the advice of an English teacher that music suited him best and he headed for the 'big time' in Los Angeles. Frey meanwhile was trying to use some of his songs as a wedge for a solo career and got the chance to play some to David Geffen, then manager of Joni Mitchell and Crosby, Stills, Nash & Young. Geffen discouraged the solo approach and told Frey to join a band. Heeding this, Frey accepted a job with Linda Ronstadt, and as the band needed a drummer he looked up Henley. The two proved highly compatible, and on the first night of the Ronstadt tour they agreed to start their own band. The band, in effect, took shape around them. Ronstadt's manager, John Boylan, brought in Randy Meisner on bass guitar and also recruited Bernie Leadon on lead guitar.

Helped by strong recommendation from Jackson Browne, the group got Geffen as their first manager and he financed the band so they could move to Aspen, Colorado, to rehearse, write songs, and polish their act in local clubs. Meanwhile, Geffen managed to get Frey a release from Amos Records and lined up a recording contract with Asylum. In early 1972, he arranged for the band to go to England to work on their debut LP under the direction of veteran producer Glyn Johns. The first fruit of that was the hit single "Take It Easy", written by Browne and Frey and issued in early summer 1972. In July 1972 their first album, EAGLES, was released.

In 1973, the band went back into London's Olympia studios to work on their second album. It was an ambitious project, a concept album with all the songs tied into the theme of the rise and·fall of the Doolin-Dalton gang of Wild West fame. Called DESPERADO it came out in the spring of 1973 and was only moderately successful. The lukewarm reception to the LP stirred unease among some admirers, fearing The Eagles might go the way of Poco and the Burritos. Adding to that were reports of internal dissension and later, of arguments with Johns about the next LP. The band decided to switch from Geffen to Irving Azoff for management, with Bill Szymczyk moving in as producer. In the process the band found a fifth member, Don Felder - one of the best slide guitarists in pop music. When the album ON THE BORDER was released it was announced that Felder had become The Eagles' fifth member.

Rumours persisted about internal problems as the months went by. In 1975 "One of These Nights" was released and went well past platinum levels. By the end of 1975, Leadon indicated he had become tired of the touring grind and the pressures of band life and wanted out. His place was taken in early 1976 by Joe Walsh. Also managed by Azoff, Walsh was an excellent guitarist, singer and songwriter, who had been a member of the James Gang and later a successful solo artist.

The LP HOTEL CALIFORNIA combined unique insights with first-rate musicianship on every track. Among the singles hits culled from it were gems such as the title song and "New Kid In Town". But another personnel shift was on the agenda: Randy Meisner departed during 1979 to seek a solo career - his place was taken by bass guitarist Timothy B Schmidt, a former member of Poco. The new line-up completed the next album, THE LONG RUN, in the autumn of '79. The LP went platinum and provided three top 10 singles, "Heartache Tonight", the title song, and "I Can't Tell You Why". In the early 1980s, the two prime writing forces, Henley and Frey, began work on solo albums and due to their efforts towards these projects, The Eagles was disbanded in May 1982.

In the spring of 1987 there were rumours about a reunion, but that didn't happen until early 1994 when Henley, Frey and Walsh met to talk about this possibility. The result was a world tour and a new album HELL FREEZES OVER, with four new songs and 11 live tracks including a superb acoustic version of "Hotel California".

Performance Notes

Hotel California

A seventies classic, renowned for it's multiple of layers of guitar, which build more and more as the song progresses. At the beginning, the main part is taken by a twelve string acoustic with a capo at the seventh fret. This is soon joined by a quieter melody, played on six string guitar and by the time the first chorus comes around there are more still. Each verse and chorus brings a new part.

The climax of the song is when the first solo begins, using a natural sounding valve overdrive - probably a Fender Twin reverb. The two lead guitars swap solos using several interesting tricks such as bending two strings at once to achieve the sound of one note raising up then another coming down - also sliding along one string to make whole segments of the melody.

Like many seventies records, some of the solo work here is played through a phase-shifter giving some of the playing a very liquid sound.

The solo work is all based around the B minor pentatonic scale (B,D,E,F#,A) incorporating occasional notes to fit with certain chords; eg when the F# major chord comes in for the first time the solo guitar plays a Bb to fit perfectly over the chord which contains a Bb. This approach is known as 'playing over the changes' and involves thinking not so much what key you are in, but what chord you are in, using the overall context of the B minor pentatonic. The famous harmonies follow the harmony of the backing chords very closely, but great care should be taken to keep the phrasing 'tight' between the two harmony guitars.

Life In The Fast Lane

This song is played with an overdrive sound - though not too over driven - and was probably played on a Gibson Les Paul through one of Joe Walsh's hot-rodded Fender Twin Reverb amplifiers. The main theme is introduced, then doubled an octave higher. As with all harmony or doubling work it is important to keep the phrasing identical on the two guitars.

During the verse a multitude of guitars play different parts. The key to using this approach is not to allow any one part to be too loud in the nix, but to link with the others equally in the listener's mind. Later in the song some heavy riffing happens, based around an E chord - accented by the drums and the rest of the band. The solo is played using a slide or bottleneck - remember when using a slide to play directly above the fret required and always mute behind the slide, to stop the sound from becoming messy. The solo work is based around the B major pentatonic scale, but uses several 'chromatic passing tones' - notes which fit in a faster context to join ideas but not when sustained individually.

One Of These Nights

An atmospheric introduction on bass and guitar, layering up different parts leads to a sudden harmony part played on another pair of guitars (this part could be played on one guitar). The general feel of the track is very funky, with minimalistic work from a clean rhythm guitar. The harmony guitars join in occasionally for an embellishment.

The solo is played with an overdriven sound and a funky style again. It may take some practice to execute some of these phrases perfectly at first, especially in succession, or even two bent notes as happens quite early in the solo which uses the E minor pentatonic scale (E,G,A,B,D), however to follow a more melodic path some notes are added especially to fit with certain chords; eg a C is used over the A minor chord which contains A,C and E. It would be possible to solo over the chords without adding these extra notes, but would not sound as interesting. Overall, it's important to keep short notes and chords in this track percussive - maybe even exaggerating this until it comes naturally.

Tequila Sunrise

Beginning with acoustic guitar - soon joined by a clean electric playing bent notes and double stops through a slight tremelo effect - this part is quite inventive in it's use of string bends and though it requires practice to play this kind of part smoothly, it is very rewarding. The solo section is played on acoustic guitar using double stops over open strings making this a solo that could possibly stand on its own with no backing! It is based around the G major scale (G,A,B,C,D,E,F#,G) with some chromatic movement (movement by steps) between the notes of the scale.

New Kid In Town

Played on both 'clean' and 'distorted' guitars, with back up from a strummed acoustic, there are a variety of different parts here. The clean guitar plays a mixture of double stops and arpeggiated chords (probably a Fender Telecaster through a Fender Twin Reverb amp). While the distorted guitar joins with some surprise accents in the chorus. Interestingly, the song is in the key of E major for the verse, and E minor for the chorus. Fills are based around the E major pentatonic scale (E,F#,G#,B,C#).

As with "One Of These Nights" there are occasions when the chord work needs to be really crisp, in this case a direct contrast from the flowing arpeggiated chords. Towards the end of the track, the clean guitar plays a chiming part which stays constant over changing chords. Generally speaking, a versatile approach is required for this versatile song.

Lyin' Eyes

A mellow sounding track, with acoustic guitar backing throughout, punctuated with various fills on electric guitar. Many of the fills use the double-stop and string bending techniques, to create a sound not unlike a pedal steel guitar. This is probably better described as 'warmth' almost certainly the result of playing a clean valve amplifier (probably a Fender Twin Reverb) at volume.

The solo guitars also descends chromatically from one chord to another - a fret at a time - on occasion. This lends a country feel to the overall sound. Generally this songs needs to sound as effortless as possible! This track is in the key of G.

Take It Easy

This track is underpinned by acoustic guitar throughout - later being joined by banjo, in the country tradition! but one thing that is very noticeable about this song is the chiming, chorused embellishment probably played on a Fender Telecaster, through a Fender Twin Reverb amplifier. Another traditional country trick to appear in this song are the 'double-stops' frequently used by the lead guitar. The important thing to remember about these, if one of the notes is to be bent, is to keep the other note or notes absolutely static rather than allowing them to drift sharp. This is particularly relevant to the fill which joins the track with the drums, making it a great exercise for building fretting hand strength. This part is based around the G major pentatonic scale (G,A,B,D,E). In the main part of the song the lead guitar plays arpeggiated chords along with the strummed acoustic - this was probably improvised originally, but is reproduced note for note here. If you do decide to play this part in an improvised manner, take care not to let it become too busy.

Best Of My Love

Performed over a lush backing of acoustic twelve-string, the solo guitar part was originally played on a pedal steel guitar, which is often heard in country music. However, it can be played on electric guitar using a bottleneck or slide, to almost identical effect. The scale used is the C major pentatonic (C,D,E,G,A). An important ingredient of the sound here is lots of reverb, and as always when playing slide, mute behind the slide - positioning it directly over the required frets. Also try keeping the guitar's tone knob down low. This should be played with a warn, clean tone.

Notation & Tablature explained

BEND: Strike the note and bend up a whole step (two frets)

BEND: Strike the note and bend up a half step (one fret)

BEND AND RELEASE: Strike the note, bend up a half step, then release the bend.

PRE-BEND: Bend the note up, then strike it

PRE-BEND AND RELEASE: Bend up, strike the note, then release it

QUARTER-TONE BEND: Bend the note slightly sharp

UNISON BEND: Strike both notes, then bend the lower note up to the pitch of the higher one

TREMOLO BAR BENDS: Strike the note, and push the bar down and up by the amounts indicated

HAMMER-ON: Strike the first note, then sound the second by fretting it without picking

PULL-OFF: Strike the higher note, then pull the finger off while keeping the lower one fretted

SLIDE: Slide the finger from the first note to the second. Only the first note is struck

SLIDE: Slide to the fret from a few frets below or above

VIBRATO: The string is vibrated by rapidly bending and releasing a note with the fretboard hand or tremolo bar

TAPPING: Hammer on to the note marked with a T using the picking hand, then pull off to the next note, following the hammer-ons or pull-offs in the normal way

NATURAL HARMONIC: Lightly touch the string directly over the fret shown, then strike the note to create a "chiming" effect

ARTIFICIAL HARMONIC: Fret the note, then use the picking hand finger to touch the string at the position shown in brackets and pluck with another finger

ARTIFICIAL HARMONIC: The harmonic is produced by using the edge of the picking hand thumb to "pinch" the string whilst picking firmly with the plectrum

PALM MUTES: Rest the palm of the picking hand on the strings near the bridge to produce a muted effect. Palm mutes can apply to a single note or a number of notes (shown with a dashed line)

Hotel California

Words and Music by DON FELDER, DON HENLEY and GLENN FREY

Verse 2:

There she   stood in the door - way,   I heard the mis - sion bell——.   An' I was think-in' to my - self—— this could be

heav - en or this could be   hell——.   Then she lit up a can - dle——.   an' she   showed me the way——.

time— of year—— (an-y time— of year——) you can' find— it here—.

Rhythm guitar continues sim.

Verse 3:

Her mind is tif-fa-ny twist-ed.   She got the Mer-ce des— bends—. (Uh)

She got a lot of pret- ty, pret- ty boys—, that she calls friends———. How they dance in the court- yard,

sweet——— sum- mer sweat. Some dance to re- mem- ber——, some dance to for - get—.

Verse 4:

17

An' still those voic - es are call - ing from far a - way

Wake you up in the mid - dle of the night —, just to hear them — say —.

Guitar Solos:

(Electric 6-String)

Soloist 2 (Don Felder)

(Soloist 1 plays upper part)

Outro:

Life In The Fast Lane

Words and Music by JOE WALSH, DON HENLEY and GLENN FREY

He was a

Verse 1:

hard-head-ed man——, he was bru-tal-ly hand-some, an' she was ter-mi-nal-ly pret-ty.

She held him up and he held her for ran - som in the heart—

of the cold—, cold—— cit - y.   He had a   nas - ty rep - u - ta - tion as a

33

out - ra - geous par - ties, they paid heav - en - ly bills_____. They were lines_____ on the mir - or, lines— on her face.   She pre-tend-ed not to no-tice,   she was   caught up in the   race—.

Out in the eve-nin',   un-til   it was light,   he was   too   tired   to   make it, she was

Verse 3:

Blow - in' and burn - in'   blind - ed by thirst——,   they——

—— did - n't see the stop   sign——, took a turn——   for the worst——.   She said,   "lis - ten, ba - by,   you can

got to pay him cash___." They went rush - in' down___ that free way, mess a - round an' got___ lost_____, they did-n't care, they were just dy-in' to get off an' it was

Chorus:

Life in the fast lane.

Sure-ly make you lose your mind. *Life in the fast lane.* Hm, hm.

Ev-'ry-thing all the time,

44

Life in the fast___ lane___.

Guitar 1 (flanged)

Guitar 3 (flanged)

Life in the fast___ lane___.

Guitar 1 continues rhythm figure 1 simile to end.

One Of These Nights

Words and Music by GLENN FREY and DON HENLEY

Verse 1:

we're gon-na find—— out—— pret - ty ma - ma——, what turns on——

—— your lights——. The full—— moon is call - in', the

(Lead Guitars)

div.

fe - ver is high—— an' the wick - ed wind whis - pers and moans——.

You got your de - mons, you got de - sires——, well, I—— got a few of my own——.

Chorus:

Oo, some - one to be kind to— in be - tween the dark and the light—

—, oo, come - in' right be - hind you,

(Lead Guitars) div.

Am   Bm7

swear I'm gon-na find you___ one of these nights___. One of these___

Verse 2: (All guitars as Verse 1)

Em   Em/D   Cmaj7

dreams___, one of these___ lost and lone-ly dreams___, now___, we're gon-na

Am   Em   Bm

find__ one__, mm__, one that real-ly screams___. I've been

Em   Em7   Em/D

search-in' for the daugh-ter of the de-vil him-self___, I've been

Cmaj7   Am

search-in' for an an-gel in white___: (An') I've been wait-in' for a wo-man who's a

Em   Em7   Em   Bm7

lit-tle of both___ an' I can feel her but she's no-where in sight___.

Chorus:

Oo, lon - li - ness will blind you—— in be - tween the wrong and the right——

let ring

; oh————————! oo, com - in' right be - hind you—,

let ring————

(Lead Guitars) div.

swear I'm gon - na find you⎯⎯⎯ one of these nights⎯⎯⎯.

Chorus:

nights _____ , mm _____ , in be - tween the dark and the light

die_____, guess I'll die_____ been all a - lone_____.
One of these_____

nights_____ . One of these cra -

zy cra - zy, cra - zy nights_____
One of these

nights

Swear I'm gon - na find—— you, com - in' right be - hind me, now——
One of these——

——. Hoo——

nights——

Tequila Sunrise

Words and Music by DON HENLEY and GLENN FREY

$\quad \bullet = 116$

Easy mid-tempo country

Verse 1:

said good bye———.

He was just a hir - ed hand———, work - ing on the

Chorus:

Verse 2:
with rhythm figure 1 & 1a

She was-n't just an-oth-er wom-an, and I could-n't

keep from com-in' on———. It's been so long———

Bridge:

Take an-oth-er shot of cour - age, won - der why the

right words___ nev - er___ come___ , you just get___ numb___

___. It's an - oth - er Te - qui - la Sun - rise

73

this old world —— still —— looks the same ——, an-oth-er frame——

Guitar 1 (Acoustic)

Guitar 2 (Electric)

Guitar 3 (Acoustic)

New Kid In Town

Words and Music by DAVID JOHN SOUTHER, DON HENLEY and GLENN FREY

Verse 1:

There's talk on the street—— it sounds—— so fa - mil - iar——.

Guitar 1 (Acoustic)

Guitar 2 (Electric)

Guitar 3 (Keyboard arr.)

they all____ seem____ to know____ you____.

Guitar 3 (Keyboard arr.)

E - ven your old____ friends treat you like you're some - thing new____.

Guitar 1 (Acoustic)

Guitar 2 (Electric)

Let ring -

Guitar 3 (Keyboard arr.)

80

84

There's so man - y

Guitar 3 (Keyboard arr.)

hold——— her.   Tears——— on   your   shoul - der.

Verse 3:

There's   talk   on   the   street   it's   there   to - re - mind——— you

Guitar 1 (Acoustic)

Continued simile

Guitar 2 (Electric)

Guitar 4 (Electric)

Chorus:

Where you— been late - ly?

(with distortion)

There's a new kid— in— town.

Ev - 'ry - bod - y

just an - oth - er new kid in town

Guitar 2 (Electric)

Oo—— hoo. Ev - 'ry - bod - y's talk - in' 'bout the new kid in town.

Oo——— hoo.   Ev - 'ry - bod - y's talk - in' 'bout the

new kid   in town.   There's a   new kid   in   town.

Guitar 2 (Electric)

Guitar 3 (Keyboard arr.)

I   don't wan - na   hear it. There's a   new kid in town.   I——— don't wan - na   hear it. Ah -

94

There's a new kid in town. Ev - 'ry - bod - y's talk - in'. There's a new kid in town. peo - ple start - ed walk - in'. There's a new kid in town. Hm——,

hm There's a new kid in town. Hm, hm, hm——————————,

Lyin' Eyes

Words and Music by DON HENLEY and GLENN FREY

Verse 1:

Cit - y   girls—   just   seem   to   find—   out   ear - ly—

how   to   o - pen—   doors—   with   just   a—   smile—

Verse 3:

he knows where   she's   go - in' as she's   leav - in———.

she is head - ed for——   the cheat - in'   side—— of town

ain't no way—— to hide—— your ly - in' eyes——.

Verse 6:

She gets up___ an' pours___ her-self___ a strong___ one,

an' stares out at the stars___ up in the___ sky___

Verse 7: (Enter Mandolin)

she's so far gone she feels just like a fool

My, oh, my, you sure know how to ar- range things,

you set it____ up so well____ so____ care - ful -

ly_____. Ain't it fun - ny how your new

Take It Easy

Words and Music by JACKSON BROWNE and GLENN FREY

♩ = *138*

Moderate Country feel

Verse 1:

Well I'm a run-nin' down the road try'n' to loos-en my load, I've got sev-

— en wom-en on my mind, four that wan-na own me, two

that wan - na stone me____, one____ says she's a friend____ of mine____. Take it____ eas -

y, take it____ eas -

don't e - ven try—— to un - der - stand——, just find a

place to make—— your—— stand—— an' take it eas

Let ring

y _____.   Well,   I'm   a

Verse 2:

stand - in'   on   a   cor - ner   in   Win - slow,   Ar - i - zo - na_____   an'   such   a   fine_____ sight_____ to   see_____

Let ring

Acoustic Guitar Continues Sim

it's a girl my Lord, in a flat bed Ford slow - in'

Let ring

(Electric Guitar)

down to take a look at me. Come on ba - by,

Let ring

We may lose_____ and we may_____ win, though we will

nev - er be here_____ a - gain_____, so o - pen up I'm climb - in' in

Let ring------------------------ Let ring----------

so take it eas   y

Guitar Solo:

(Enter Banjo)

Verse 3:

run - nin' down the road try'in' to loos - en my load_____, got a world_____

(Rhythm Guitar)

_____ of trou - ble on my_____ mind, look - in' for a lov - er who won't blow my cov - er, she's so———— hard to find————.   Take it—— eas -

y,   take it——— eas

y,   don't let the sound of your___ own___ wheels_____ make you

cra - zy___.   Come on___ ba - by_____,

don't— say— may - be, I———— got - ta

know if your— sweet— love— is gon - na save———————— me———.

Outro:

Oo_____, Oo_____, Oo_____.

Oh_____, we got it eas

We ought to take it

eas

Best Of My Love

Words and Music by DAVID JOHN SOUTHER, DON HENLEY and GLENN FREY

Verse 2:

left us so lit - tle to give_____. That same old_____ crowd_____ was like a

cold dark cloud_____ that we could nev - er rise_____ a - bove_____.

But here in my heart—— I give you the best—— of my——

Chorus:

love.

Whoa——————,   sweet— dar -

Bridge:

be al - right   if I could   go_____   on   sleep - ing.   But

Verse 3:

ev - 'ry morn - in'   I . wake up an' wor - ry_____   what's gon - na   hap - pen   to - day_____

You see it your___ way an' I see it mine___ but we

both see it slipp-in' a-way___. You know we al-ways had each

sweet dar - lin'. - you get the best of my love.

love.

love. the best of my love.

Oh sweet dar - lin', ev - 'ry night an' day,

Printed by Halstan & Co. Ltd., Amersham, Bucks., England